HOW TO BE AN INVENTOR

by Murray Suid

Illustrated by Mike Artell

This book is for
Eric Dorsey

Publisher: Roberta Suid
Design: David Hale
Copy Editor: Carol Whiteley
Typesetting: Santa Monica Press
Production: Susan Pinkerton
Consultants: Catherine Dilts and Cathy Chowenhill

Also in this series: *How to Be President of the U.S.A.*

Other books by the author: *Book Factory, Editing,
Greeting Cards, Letter Writing, More Book Factory,
Picture Book Factory, Report Factory, Research,
Sentences, Stories, Writing Hangups, Ten-Minute
Thinking Tie-ins, Ten-Minute Whole Language Warm-ups,
Cooperative Language Arts, Cooperative Research and Reports*

Concept for videophone illustration, page 68, courtesy CLI

CONTENTS

INTRODUCTION 4

Part 1. LEARN THE BASICS 5
Be Inventive 6
Take an Invention Quiz 7
Invention Quiz Answers 8
The Steps of Invention 9
Keep an Inventor's Diary 11
Leonardo da Vinci's Journal 12
Wilbur Wright's Diary 13
Read About Inventors 14
Unfamous Inventors 15
Trace an Invention 16
The Ever-changing Bike 17
Hunt for Inventions 18
What's in a Baseball? 19
Interview an Inventor 20

Part 2. SHARPEN YOUR SKILLS 21
Learn to Draw 22
Convertible Skate-Shoes 23
Take Things Apart 24
Take-Apart Project 25
Be a Fact Finder 26
A Famous Letter 27
Do Science 28
The Scientific Method 29
Practice Teamwork 30
Teamwork Tips 31
Name It 32
Name Game 33
Be a Critical Thinker 34
Invention Evaluation Form 35
Learn from Failure 36
Persistence Pays 37
Be Handy 38

Part 3. GET IDEAS 39
Learn from Animals 40
Birds and the Airplane 41
Be a People Watcher 42
Problem Solvers 43

Enjoy Surprises 44
The Slinky Story 45
Think Up Wild Ideas 46
Wild Inventions 47
Recycle Things 48
What Can You Do with an Egg? 49
Imitate Nature 50
Know the News 51
Collect Complaints 52

Part 4. INVENT FOR REAL 53
Invent Add-on Gadgets 54
Bells and Whistles 55
Design Something 56
Sample Designs 57
Invent a Game 58
Game Planner 59
Invent a Method 60
Two Amazing Methods 61
Invent a Business 62
Business Planner 63
Invent a Character 64
The Invention of Santa Claus 65
Borrow an Invention 66
From Horseback to the Moon 67
Improve an Invention 68
Invent a Group 69
Invent a Toy 70

Part 5. SHARE YOUR IDEAS 71
Learn About Patents 72
Page from the Slinky Patent 73
Apply for a Patent 74
A Stirring and Eating Tool 75
Patent Facts and Tips 76

Resources
Inventor's Address Book 77
Reading List 78
Teacher Tips 79
Index 80

INTRODUCTION

Anyone can be an inventor! All it takes is desire and the effort to master a few basic skills, such as observing and experimenting.

Most people are inventors without even knowing it. Finding a new way to play an old game is an invention. So is taking a different way to school, or rigging up a gadget to make a chore easier. A story with an unexpected twist is a kind of invention. So is a tune never heard before or a new recipe for pancakes.

This book aims to help inventors strengthen their natural creativity. It presents tips and secrets that successful inventors know, for example, that it's possible to learn as much from a failure as from a success.

The book has six parts:

• **Learn the Basics** covers what inventing is all about.

• **Sharpen Your Skills** shows how to practice drawing, researching, brainstorming, and other activities which make invention possible.

• **Get Ideas** explains a variety of ways for thinking up inventions, including people watching, recycling, and borrowing from nature.

• **Invent for Real** gives tips for creating gadgets, methods, toys, games, characters, and designs.

• **Share Your Ideas** deals with patenting and bringing your inventions to the public.

• **Resources** offers a bibliography, an address list (which includes news about invention contests), and—for the teacher—whole class projects, such as making an invention time line.

Stories about inventions fill the pages, from Ben Franklin's armonica to Virginia Apgar's system for saving newborns. The Wright brothers are mentioned often because their approach is a model for independent inventing. While we might not all be as successful as the inventors honored here, we can learn from them and amaze ourselves with our own creativity.

Important Safety Note!
Inventors deal with the unknown. What we don't know can hurt us. The best inventors take care to avoid injuring themselves or others. When in doubt, stop and ask an expert.

PART 1

LEARN THE BASICS

Nothing in life is to be feared.
It is only to be understood.
Marie Curie

BE INVENTIVE

Inventors come from both rich and poor families. They live in every part of the world. Some are highly educated. Others have spent little time in school. Despite these differences, inventors share many of the following qualities.

Try this: *Check your inventive qualities. Add more if you like.*

	I'M LIKE THIS ALREADY	I WANT TO BE MORE LIKE THIS
Confident: I believe in my ideas even if other people think they're silly.	☐	☐
Cooperative: I'm good at teamwork.	☐	☐
Curious: I'm interested in figuring out why things work or don't work.	☐	☐
Handy: I like to make or fix things, and enjoy learning to use hammers, saws, computers, and other tools.	☐	☐
Imaginative: I like to think up ideas.	☐	☐
Observant: I notice details that other people might overlook.	☐	☐
Persistent: I work until a job is done.	☐	☐

Bonus: *Contact an inventor by letter or phone. Ask the person to describe his or her qualities.*

TAKE AN INVENTION QUIZ

No one is born knowing how to invent things. However, you can learn how to do it, just like learning how to play a musical instrument or be a teacher. Here's a chance to find out how much you already know about this important kind of work.

Try this: *Decide if the following statements are "True" or "False."*

	TRUE	FALSE
1. Inventions have at least one moving part.	☐	☐
2. An invention is something that has never been seen before.	☐	☐
3. Most things that we use today were invented in the last 100 years.	☐	☐
4. Many inventions are created by several people working as a team.	☐	☐
5. Inventors own their ideas forever.	☐	☐
6. Most inventions are worth a lot of money.	☐	☐
7. Inventors need a college education.	☐	☐
8. Writers have thought up some inventions.	☐	☐
9. People who invent popular products usually become very famous.	☐	☐
10. The most difficult part of being an inventor is getting an idea for an invention.	☐	☐

★INVENTION QUIZ ANSWERS★

1. FALSE. Many inventions, such as paper, have no moving parts.

2. FALSE. Most inventions improve earlier things. For example, black and white television was invented in 1928, color television came in 1949.

3. FALSE. Examples of things over a century old include paper, electric lights, fireworks, kites, mirrors, soap, wheels, eyeglasses, and writing.

4. TRUE. Teams invented well-known inventions including the airplane and the personal computer. In some cases, one person got the credit although several people worked on the project. This is true of many of Thomas Edison's inventions.

5. FALSE. If the government decides that an invention is new, the inventor gets a patent. This gives sole use of the invention for a set time, usually 17 years. After that, anyone may use the idea.

6. FALSE. While some inventions are worth millions of dollars, others have no worth. Examples include: a fly swatter gun and a robot swimming coach.

7. FALSE. Thomas Edison, Wilbur Wright, and other inventors didn't even graduate from high school. However, education often gives inventors important skills. For example, Robert Goddard, inventor of the rocket engine, had a Ph.D. degree in physics. He used his scientific knowledge to figure out how to use high-energy fuels.

8. TRUE. For example, in 1898 H. G. Wells described a laser-like "heat ray" in his science fiction novel, *War of the Worlds*. The real laser beam was invented in 1958.

9. FALSE. Many inventors of famous products are unfamous. For example, can you name the inventors of the ball-point pen, drive-in movie, miniature golf, neon light, potato chip, safety pin, tea bag, Velcro, and zipper? (The answers are given throughout this book.)

10. FALSE. Often the idea for an invention comes suddenly, but making a working model takes much effort. For example, the Wright brothers studied and experimented for more than four years before they flew their first motorized airplane.

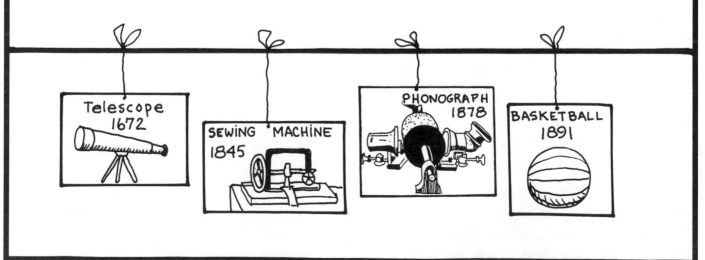

Telescope 1672

SEWING MACHINE 1845

PHONOGRAPH 1878

BASKETBALL 1891

★THE STEPS OF INVENTION★

No two inventors work exactly the same way. However, most go through some or all of the seven steps shown here. To make the steps easy to follow, the word "inventor" is used. In reality, two or more people often work as an inventing team.

1. Problem: The inventor wants to solve a problem or answer a question. For example, Eadweard Muybridge wondered: Does a horse ever have all its feet off the ground? The question led Muybridge to invent a motion picture machine. The device proved that horses can "fly."

2. Idea: The inventor imagines a way to solve the problem. The inventor needs confidence because people may say that the idea is crazy. For example, just days before the Wright brothers flew their first airplane, a scientist wrote that airplanes wouldn't be invented for a million years.

3. Background research: An inventor learns what others know about the problem. For example, Italian Guglielmo Marconi read about an English experiment that had the missing idea needed to invent radio.

★THE STEPS OF INVENTION★

4. Plan: The inventor describes the invention in words or pictures. Like an outline for a story, this description helps the inventor build the actual invention.

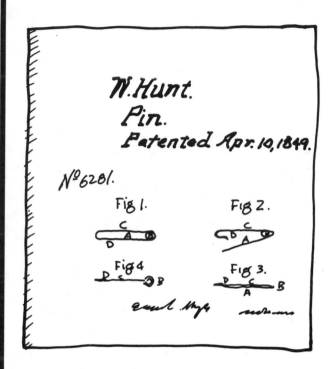

5. Creation: The inventor builds a working model of the invention. Sometimes it takes only a few hours, as with the invention of the safety pin. More often, this step involves trial and error. For example, it took the Nestle company from 1931 to 1938 to find the formula for instant coffee.

6. Field testing: The inventor tries the invention under real conditions. For example, Robert Goddard, father of the modern rocket, spent years launching rockets. He learned from both his successes and failures.

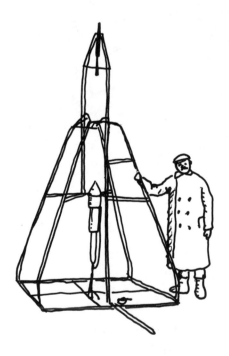

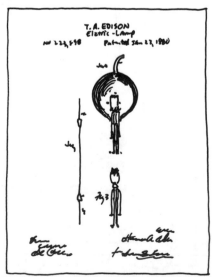

7. Patent: To patent the idea so that no one else can use it, the inventor sends a detailed report to the government. If experts agree that the idea is new, the inventor gets to own it for a certain number of years.

KEEP AN INVENTOR'S DIARY

Ideas are easy to forget. That's why many inventors hold onto their thoughts by writing and drawing in diaries or journals. Every drawing or note is called an entry.

Try this: *Begin your own inventor's diary. Use it for the activities in this book as well as for your own inventions. You'll find that the more you use your diary, the more ideas you'll get.*

TIPS FOR KEEPING A DIARY

1. If possible, use a notebook with bound-in pages rather than a loose-leaf notebook. Pages are less likely to be lost this way.

2. Fill the diary with anything that relates to your inventing work:
   • ideas for inventions
   • observations
   • drawings and diagrams
   • questions to answer

3. Date everything that you write or draw in your journal. If you write several entries on one day, date each one. When you have an idea for a really important invention, have two people outside your family sign their names next to it and add the date. Diary dates can help you prove when you first had an idea. This can be important when two or more people claim the same invention.

4. Start at the beginning and fill each page in order. If you want to say more about an idea you entered earlier, add the idea on the new page and include a note that refers to the earlier entry.

5. Keep your diary in a safe place at home. To capture ideas when you're somewhere else, carry a smaller notebook or write your ideas on note cards. You can then copy these notes into your diary.

Bonus: *Study other inventors' notebooks. You can find examples in library books about famous inventors.*

★LEONARDO DA VINCI'S JOURNAL★

Leonardo da Vinci was an Italian artist and inventor who lived from 1452 until 1519. His "Mona Lisa" is one of the world's best known paintings. But da Vinci's notebooks are also famous. Although he lived centuries before modern engines were invented, da Vinci drew plans for the helicopter and other wonders. He often added words explaining his ideas. You may have trouble reading his text because it's in Italian. Also, for unknown reasons, da Vinci wrote backwards (mirror writing).

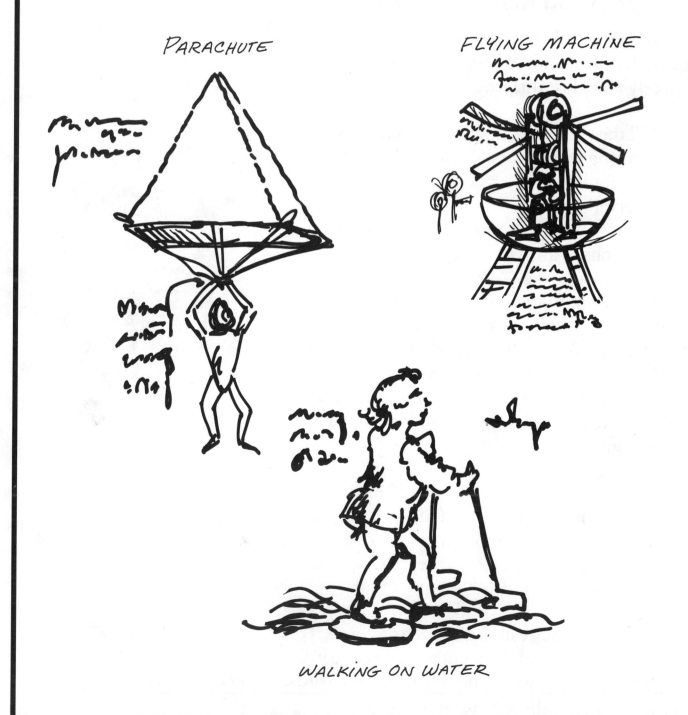

PARACHUTE

FLYING MACHINE

WALKING ON WATER

★THE EVER-CHANGING BIKE★

1791: The "wooden horse," invented in France by Comte de Sivrac, had a fixed front wheel, and couldn't easily be steered. Riders pushed their feet on the ground to make it go.

1839: Kirkpatrick Macmillan's "foot treadle" bicycle used levers to drive the rear wheel. The steerable front wheel was attached to an iron fork fitted to a wooden frame. Scotland's Macmillan is considered the "father" of the modern bicycle.

1870s: "High bicycles," also called "Penny-farthings," were developed by inventors in France, England, and the U.S. The huge front wheel allowed cyclists to go fast, but they often fell off these unstable machines.

1880s: Many inventors worked on chain-driven "safety bicycles." This design became the standard for many years.

1980: "Recumbent bicycles," developed in the U.S., allow riders to pedal with great force. Average cyclists can now reach speeds of over 50 miles per hour (80 kilometers per hour).

HUNT FOR INVENTIONS

Painters look at paintings, and musicians listen to music. In the same way, inventors spend time studying inventions. By paying attention to products other people have created, you'll begin to think like an inventor yourself.

Try this: *Take an invention safari. See how many inventions you use in a day or a week. Write your observations in your inventor's diary. If you keep your eyes open, you'll probably be able to list hundreds of things that were invented either long ago or just last year.*

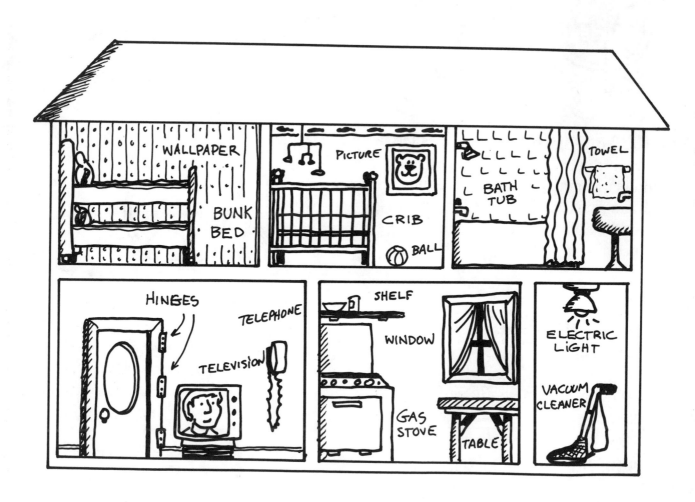

Bonus: *Choose an object or an invention that has at least four or five parts. Examples include: a shoe, a toaster, a light bulb, or a traffic light. Do library research to discover the history of each part that makes up the whole thing.*

★WHAT'S IN A BASEBALL?★

The game of baseball became popular in the United States in the nineteenth century. Abner Doubleday is sometimes given credit for inventing the game in 1839. However, baseball actually grew from two English games: cricket and rounders.

The ball used in baseball brings together many inventions. Some of them are thousands of years old.

Leather: About 15,000 years ago, cave dwellers learned how to turn animal skins into leather (tanning).

Sewing: The oldest needles, made of bone, are five thousand years old. The kind of thread used in a baseball was invented in the 1770s.

Alphabet: The alphabetic writing on a baseball came from the Phoenicians five thousand years ago.

Printing: Two thousand years ago, the Chinese learned to use presses to print words. About 500 years ago European printers began using the movable-type printing press that made newspapers and books much more available than before.

Ink: Ink was invented long before presses. Three thousand years ago, in India and China, ink was made from berries and other parts of plants. Now most inks are made from chemicals.

INTERVIEW AN INVENTOR

You can learn a lot about inventing by talking to someone who works as an inventor or who invents as a hobby.

Try this: *Conduct a TV interview for a school report or to broadcast on your local public access channel.*

STEPS FOR DOING A TV INTERVIEW

1. Ask friends and neighbors if they know an inventor. You might also look in the yellow pages under "Inventors."

2. Write or phone the inventor to set up an interview. If possible, arrange to do the interview in the inventor's workshop.

3. Before the interview, list questions to ask, for example:
   - What made you want to be an inventor?
   - How do you get your ideas?
   - What do you like best and least about inventing?
   - Which of your inventions do you like best?
   - What skills do you think an inventor should have?
   - Do you work alone or with a team?
   - What advice would you give someone who wants to be an inventor?

Bonus: *Write an imaginary interview with an inventor from the past, for example, Joseph Henry, who helped develop the electromagnet, or Alice Chatham, who invented space helmets for NASA. Start by gathering facts from books. Then write a script that includes questions and answers based on your research. Publish your interview in written form, or produce it as a video play.*

PART 2

SHARPEN YOUR SKILLS

There is no substitute for hard work.
Thomas Edison

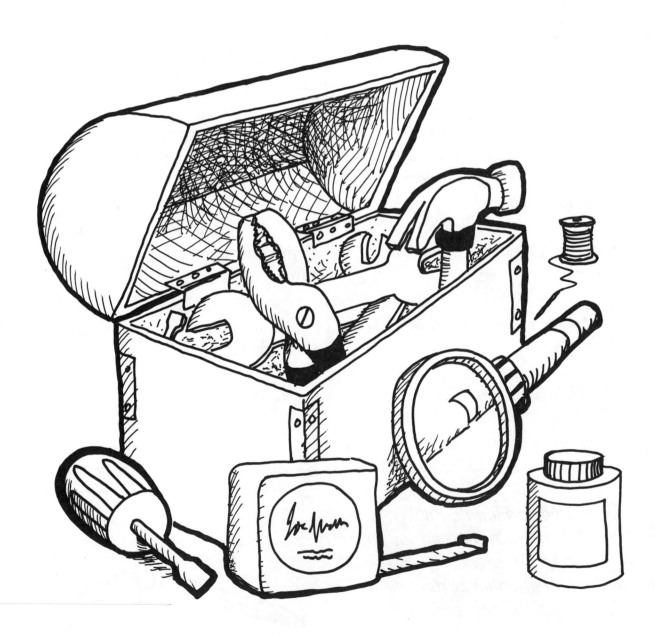

LEARN TO DRAW

Inventors use drawing in two important ways. First, they often sketch their ideas before trying to make working models. This is called "visual thinking." Like an outline for a story, a drawing can save time and effort. Second, inventors usually include sketches when applying for patents.

You don't have to be an artist to draw your ideas. The goal is simply to make your thoughts clear to yourself and to other people.

Try this: *One way to learn how to draw inventions is to look at other inventors' drawings. Study the example for "Convertible Skate-Shoes," and then answer the following questions:*

1. How many views of the object are shown?

2. What do you see in View B that's not in View A?

3. How big are the wheels?

4. Words are used in two ways. One is to name the object. What's the other?

Bonus: *Choose a familiar object, for example, a fork or a ruler. Pretend you have invented this thing. Draw two or three views of it. Number the important parts of the drawing. Then explain what each part does.*

Drawing Tips

1. Before putting anything on paper, think about what you want to show. You might state in words what you want to show. Think about how many views you'll need.

2. If you're drawing an object (and not an idea), look at it carefully before you start drawing and while you're drawing.

3. Start by drawing in pencil on scratch paper. Use a compass, a ruler, or other tools.

4. When your sketch looks right, copy it onto good paper. Make the lines clear and dark.

5. If needed, add words to clarify your ideas.

6. When you're done, study your drawing carefully. Note the parts that you like, and think about how it could be improved.

★CONVERTIBLE SKATE-SHOES★

The wheels of these skates can be raised, so that the user can walk normally in areas where skating is not allowed.

Scale: ½ inch = 2 inches

VIEW A

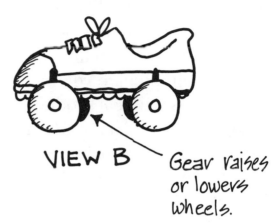

VIEW B

Gear raises or lowers wheels.

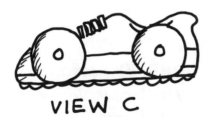

VIEW C

VIEW D

WHEELS DOWN

WHEELS UP

TAKE THINGS APART

Some inventions consist of a single thing. For example, a plastic cup is one piece of molded plastic. However, most inventions are made up of several or many parts. A toothbrush, for instance, has a handle and bristles. The space shuttle has tens of thousands of parts. Learning to see the parts of an invention can help prepare you for turning your ideas into real products.

Try this: *Get in the habit of observing objects. These might include scissors, an egg beater, a zipper, toys, a pencil sharpener, someone's hand, and pieces of fruit. With each item, see how many parts you can count. Use a magnifying glass when needed. Draw what you see and label the parts.*

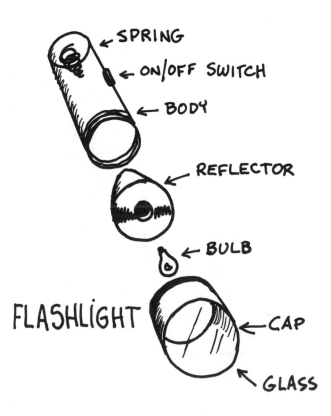

Bonus: *Practice taking apart and putting together simple objects and inventions.* <u>*For the sake of safety, check with an expert before starting this kind of project.*</u> *Work with old and unwanted things, for example, a cardboard box, a walnut, a ballpoint pen, a flashlight, eyeglasses, models, toys, a faucet, and a camera that no longer works. The secret to putting things back together again is to keep careful notes as you work. It may help to make drawings that show where the parts belong.*

A related project is to attempt to duplicate an object. An example is to make your own version of a model airplane.

★TAKE-APART PROJECT★

Manufacturers sometimes take apart and study another company's product. They may then make their own version of the thing. This is done to learn how the product works and how it was made. The activity is called "reverse engineering." You can do reverse engineering with many common objects. The steps below show how to do it with an envelope.

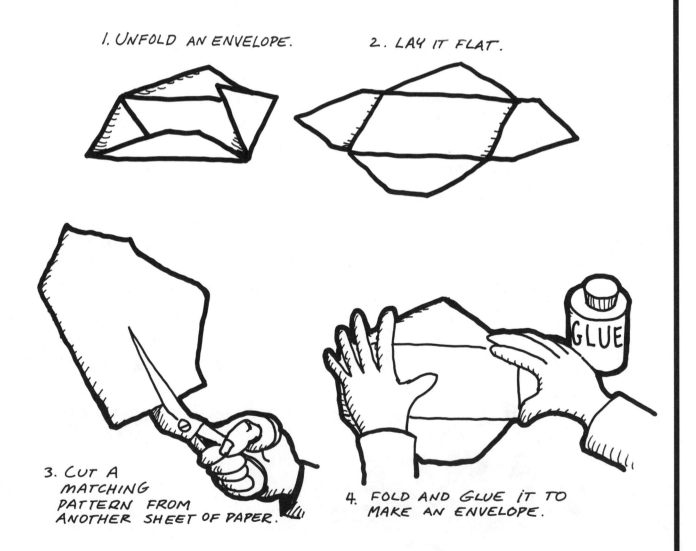

1. UNFOLD AN ENVELOPE.

2. LAY IT FLAT.

3. CUT A MATCHING PATTERN FROM ANOTHER SHEET OF PAPER.

4. FOLD AND GLUE IT TO MAKE AN ENVELOPE.

BE A FACT FINDER

Inventors are often warned: "Don't reinvent the wheel." This means not wasting time doing what others have already done. To avoid this mistake, you need to spend time reading about work in your field. Contact experts through writing, phoning, or visiting. This kind of research will help you build on the discoveries of earlier inventors. Even their failures can help guide you.

Try this: *Choose an invention that you'd like to work on, for example, a robot dog or a bike that can turn into a pedal-powered airplane. If you can't think of an idea, flip through a magazine such as* Popular Mechanics. *Then go to the library, make a list of books and articles that deal with your idea, and begin reading. Take notes on what you learn.*

A Famous Fact-finding Letter

In the 1890s, the Wright brothers read about early experiments in flight. To learn what other inventors knew, Wilbur wrote to the Smithsonian Institution. This organization helped workers in many fields, and does the same even now.

The Smithsonian answered with a list of works about flight, such as Octave Chanute's *Progress in Flying Machines* (1894) and Samuel Langley's *Experiments in Aerodynamics* (1891). They also sent pamphlets, such as Otto Lilienthal's "Practical Experiments in Soaring."

These items started the Wright brothers on a study of flight. The materials also led to pen paling with other inventors.

Bonus: *Brainstorm a list of people you could write to about your idea for an invention. For example, if you'd like to invent a robot dog, you might write to the author of a book about robots. Or you could write to a robot-making company.*

BARK.
BARK.

★A FAMOUS LETTER★

May 30, 1899

To the Smithsonian Institution
Washington, D.C.

Dear Sir:

I believe that simple flight at least is possible to man and that the experiments and investigations of a large number of independent workers will...finally lead to accomplished flight....

I am about to begin a systematic study of the subject in preparation for practical work to which I expect to devote what time I can spare from my regular business. I wish to obtain such papers as the Smithsonian Institution has published on this subject, and if possible a list of other works in print in the English language. I am an enthusiast, but not a crank in the sense that I have some pet theories as to the proper construction of a flying machine. I wish to avail myself of all that is already known and then if possible add my mite to help on the future worker who will attain final success. I do not know the terms on which you send out your publications but if you will inform me of the cost I will remit the price.

Yours,
Wilbur Wright

DO SCIENCE

There's an important difference between science and invention. Scientists try to learn the truth about animals, rainbows, stars, and other things that already exist. Inventors try to create things that don't exist.

However, the two activities often are linked. For one thing, scientists may follow up their discoveries by inventing things. After Ben Franklin scientifically studied lightning, he invented the lightning rod to protect houses.

On the other hand, inventors may need to do science while working on a project. Before they could build their first airplane, the Wright brothers needed to learn how air would lift a plane's wings. This took months of lab tests using a wind tunnel. While their goal was to invent a flying machine, much of their work was scientific.

Try this: *To sharpen your science skills, pick a subject that you can study first-hand. You might want to learn what kind of path an ant makes or what happens to a piece of fruit that's left outside.*

Famous Scientific Inventors

- Howard Aiken: automatic calculator (computer)
- Luis Alvarez: specialized radar
- Katherine Blodgett: non-reflecting glass
- George Washington Carver: many agricultural products
- Marie Curie: method for extracting polonium
- Michael Faraday: generator
- Ben Franklin: lightning rod, stove
- Galileo Galilei: telescope
- Robert Goddard: rocket
- Stephanie Kwoleck: Kelvar (material used in tires, spaceships, etc.)
- Edwin Land: Polaroid camera
- Ernest Lawrence: cyclotron
- Joseph Lister: antiseptic surgery
- Isaac Newton: calculus
- Gregor Mendel: method for breeding plants and animals
- Louis Pasteur: rabies vaccine
- Ruth Patrick: diatometer (water pollution detector)
- Alessandro Volta: battery

Bonus: *Learn more about the scientific method by reading a book about a famous scientist-inventor.*

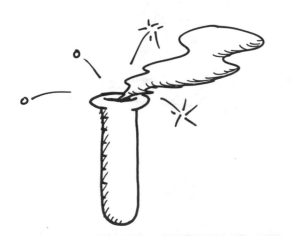

★THE SCIENTIFIC METHOD★

Choose a subject to study. It should be something that you can observe using your senses (seeing, hearing, tasting, smelling, touching) and tools, such as a magnifying glass or a camera.

Brainstorm questions that you want to answer. For example, if you plan to study goldfish, your questions might be:
- Can they see colors?
- Do they sleep?
- Do fish play together?
- Can they hear?

Choose one question that you want to focus on. Make sure it's a question that you think you can find a way to answer. For example, it might be impossible to learn what goldfish dream about.

Learn what other scientists have found out about your subject. This "background research" is often done by reading books and articles. You might also write to a scientist asking for information.

Dr. Sandy Carter
Marine Biologist
Palo Alto Aquarium
Somewhere City, CA

Decide how you will study your subject. List the materials and tools you'll be using. In some cases, you will simply observe your subject as it is and take notes on what you learn. In other cases, you might need to set up an experiment. For example, to find out if goldfish see colors, you might beam different colors at fish in their tank. When setting up an experiment, a scientist may make a prediction, such as, "Goldfish will respond more to red light than green light."

Do the study. Then, in a notebook, write and draw what you see.

Write a report about what you learned. When you share what you discovered, you make it possible for other scientists to check your work. Through reports, scientists work together to learn more about the universe.

PRACTICE TEAMWORK

Inventions are often created by people working together. For example, the light bulb was really created by a group, even though Thomas Edison got the credit. While some inventors like to work alone (and you might be one of them) it's useful to know how to be part of a team.

Try this: *Find one or more partners to work on a project. It could be a gadget, a story, a mural, a community fund-raising drive, or any other creative effort. Before beginning the real work, talk about what it takes to have a successful team.*

Some Successful Inventing Teams

- Henry Sherwin and Edward Williams: ready-mixed paint
- Steve Jobs and Steve Wozniack: Apple Computer
- Louis Downing and J. Abbott: stagecoach
- Will and John Kellogg: breakfast flakes (cereal)
- Helen Taussig and Alfred Blalock: heart surgery for newborns
- Marie Curie and Pierre Curie: method to purify radioactive ore
- Ernest Schoedsack and Merian Cooper: King Kong
- Dick and Maurice McDonald, and Ray Kroc: McDonald's
- Jerry Siegel and Joe Shuster: Superman

Bonus: *Study a famous inventing team to learn what made their partnership work. Or write to a company known for inventing products, such as airplanes, autos, chemicals, computers, household products, and movies. Ask for information about how they use teamwork. You can find their addresses in library reference books.*

★TEAMWORK TIPS★

1. Concentrate on the task, not on who gets credit.

2. Listen carefully to the other person's ideas. If you don't understand, ask questions.

3. Don't reject an idea until you've thought about it and discussed it.

4. Never make fun of a teammate's ideas. Doing so can destroy a team. Besides, sometimes silly-sounding ideas turn out to be very useful.

5. Be ready to help the other person solve a problem.

6. Share your own ideas, even those that may not work out.

7. When things go wrong, don't look for someone to blame. Focus on a solution.

8. Be aware of, and use, each other's skills and knowledge.

A Family Team

From the time we were little children my brother Orville and myself lived together, played together, worked together and, in fact, thought together. We usually owned all our toys in common, talked over our thoughts and aspirations so that nearly everything that was done in our lives has been the result of conversations, suggestions and discussions between us.

Wilbur Wright

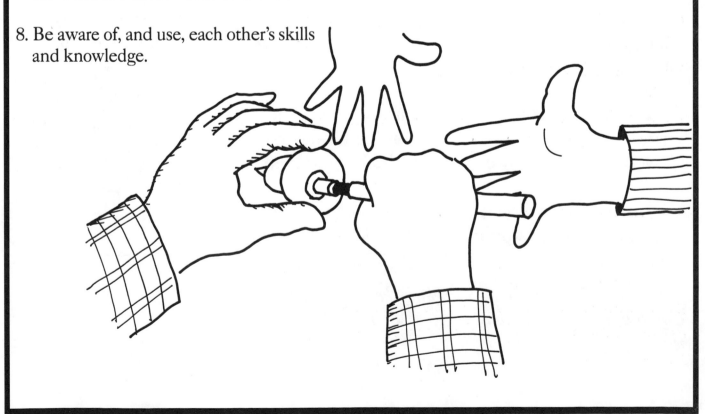

NAME IT

Shakespeare, the greatest writer of English, thought names weren't important. He wrote, "That which we call a rose by any other name would smell as sweet." Still, inventors often think carefully about invention names.

Try this: *Practice renaming familiar things in your home: bed, bicycle, book, eyeglasses, gloves, stove, television, and so on. For example, a "spoon" might be called a "souper" or a "slurper."*

Tips for Naming Products

The following name groups may give you ideas for naming products. Often an easy-to-remember or clever name can help with marketing (selling) an idea.

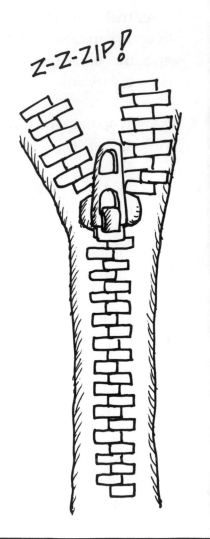

Z-Z-ZIP!

Alliteration: In a two-word name, start both words with the same sound. Example: Hula-Hoop.

Description: Tell what the product looks like or how it's made. A ball-point pen has a ball for its point.

Foreign language: Use foreign words. For example, elevator comes from the Latin word *elevare*, which means "to lift." In England, elevators are called "lifts."

Person's name: Honor the inventor or someone related to the invention. In 1910 Joshua Lionel Cowen called his new electric toy the Lionel Train.

Sound: Name the product for the sound it makes. Famous examples are Ping-Pong and zipper.

Bonus: *Learn the stories behind the names of Xerox, Cadillac, and other famous products. Start your research with the dictionary. You might also write to the public relations offices of the companies that make the products.*

★NAME GAME★

Frisbee: In the 1920s, Yale students played games using tins from the nearby Frisbie Pie Company of Bridgeport, Connecticut. Skilled tin-flippers could get the tins to do tricks, like hovering or returning to the thrower. They called the throwing games "Frisbieing" in honor of the pie company. Years later, Walt Morrison invented a similarly shaped flying toy. Someone recalled the pie tin throwing, and gave Morrison's device its now-famous name, with a slightly different spelling: the Frisbee.

Guillotine: During the French Revolution, a Dr. Joseph Guillotin spoke out in favor of a more humane method for executing criminals. The government liked the idea and chose a device called a Louisette that used a heavy blade to behead people. The Louisette was named for Dr. Antoine Louis who designed it. However, because of a song about Dr. Guillotin, people began to call the machine a "guillotine."

Braille: Louis Braille (1809-1852) was a Frenchman who was blinded in an accident when he was three. His system of reading by touching raised points was based on an earlier method invented by Charles Barbier.

Plastic: You may think of plastic as being something very hard. But the word "plastic" actually means something that can be formed. It got this name because during manufacturing, plastic is soft and can easily be molded into all sorts of shapes. The word "plastic" is very old. But the material we call plastic today was invented only about 150 years ago by an English chemist named Alexander Parkes.

Some other inventions with interesting name stories are: begonia, blimp, Chevrolet, diesel, helicopter, Jell-O, laser, Levi's, leotard, linoleum, margarine, Mercedes, pickle, praline, saxophone, television, silhouette, umbrella, vitamin, yo-yo, and zeppelin.

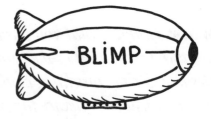

BE A CRITICAL THINKER

Most inventors hope their work will make life better for people. When this happens, it's called "progress." An example is the invention of radar, which helps planes land safely in fog.

Unfortunately, inventions that seem good at first can cause problems or be used in harmful ways. Robert Goddard invented the rocket, hoping it would lead to space exploration. But before taking astronauts to the moon, rockets were used to bomb cities.

No one can predict for sure how an invention will be used or what the bad side effects might be. Still, thoughtful inventors should at least consider the uses their ideas might be put to. If they decide that the invention will do more harm than good, they can give up the project.

Try this: *Pick an invention that you know a lot about, for example, the television, the light bulb, the bicycle, the car, dental braces, or the computer. List the invention's good points and bad points. Then decide whether or not the invention has contributed to progress.*

Inventions That Cause Harm

- Aerosol sprays
- Asbestos
- Cigarettes
- DDT insecticide
- Lawn Dart game
- PCB chemical
- Steroids to increase strength
- Supersonic transport

Bonus: *Imagine that you have an idea for an amazing invention of the future. Examples are: a time machine, clothing to make people invisible, a device for reading minds, or a robot that can do everything humans can do. Brainstorm a list of what's good and bad about that invention. Then write about why you would or wouldn't invent it.*

★INVENTION EVALUATION FORM★

Name of invention:_____

What the invention does: _____

How it helps:
( ) saves time
( ) saves labor
( ) saves money
( ) other:_____

Problems caused by the invention:
( ) noise
( ) pollution
( ) unemployment
( ) other:_____

Who is helped by the invention: _____

Who is hurt by the invention: _____

Other things or methods that could replace the invention:

_____

This invention should or should not be used because:

_____

_____

_____

_____

_____

_____

LEARN FROM FAILURE

Inventors often experience many failures before finding success. For example, when the Wright brothers began to experiment with flight, their gliders often crashed. But each disaster taught them important lessons.

Try this: *Study the story of an invention, and observe how the inventor dealt with disappointments on the way to success. You might interview a local inventor, or you might explore a famous invention such as:*

- airplane
- aspirin
- atomic bomb
- dentures
- electric light
- heart transplant
- liquid fuel rocket
- Panama Canal
- telegraph
- television
- vaccination
- vulcanized rubber

Bonus: *Think about something that you have learned to do, for example, ride a bike, play the piano, kick a football, or read a map. Write about the difficulties you encountered while mastering that skill.*

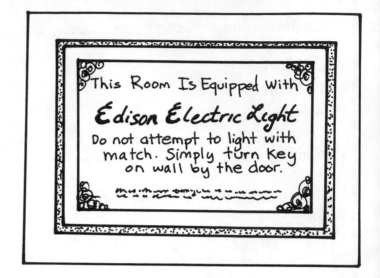

This Room Is Equipped With
Edison Electric Light
Do not attempt to light with match. Simply turn key on wall by the door.

★PERSISTENCE PAYS★

JERRY SIEGEL AND JOE SHUSTER: In 1933 two Cleveland, Ohio, teenagers came up with the idea for a new kind of comic-book hero: a visitor from another planet who could bend the strongest steel, laugh at bullets, and leap tall buildings in a single bound. They called him Superman. But all of the comic book companies rejected their stories. Finally, in 1938, a comic-book company decided to take a chance on "Superman." The first issue was a hit, and Superman went on to become the most popular hero of the time.

MCDONALD'S: In 1949, Richard and Maurice McDonald opened their first fast-food restaurant. Unlike other restaurants of the time, the menu listed only a few items. Food was served in paper containers and customers had to stand in line to get it. On opening day, only a few customers showed up. Ten year later, McDonald's had become the largest food chain in the world.

NASA: On December 6, 1957, rocket experts at Cape Canaveral attempted to launch America's first satellite aboard a Vanguard rocket. The rocket lifted twelve inches, then settled back onto the launching pad, and exploded. Newspaper writers and others questioned whether American scientists had the right stuff. Eleven and a half years later on July 20, 1969, the NASA team landed two astronauts on the moon.

RHEA ZAKICH, a housewife, temporarily lost her voice. The same thing happens to many people, but instead of complaining, Zakich invented a pantomime game she could play with her family. After "The Ungame" was rejected by 26 companies, she and a partner named Lew Herndon produced the game themselves and eventually sold more than one million copies.

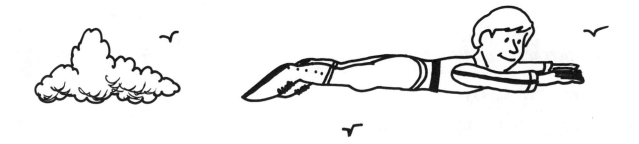

BE HANDY

To be successful, an inventor must turn a dream into reality. This means using wood, wires, or other materials to make a working model of the inventor's idea. With a simple invention, such as the safety pin, an inventor might use just one skill. With a complex invention, the work may involve dozens of skills.

Because you never know what your next idea will be, master as many crafts as you can.

Try this: *Practice being handy by creating your own versions of objects. For example:*

- *bend a paper clip into a safety pin*
- *cut and fold a piece of paper into an envelope*
- *turn a toothpick into a sewing needle*
- *sculpt a clay model of a car, a faucet, or other object.*

Hint: If possible, have a sample of the real thing in front of you to observe as you work. Also, don't expect the things you make to be as polished as those sold in stores. The goal is to gain confidence in your ability to work with different materials.

Learning by Doing

In 1887, Heinrich Hertz proved electrical energy could be sent through the air. Seven years later, as a first step in inventing radio, Guglielmo Marconi repeated Hertz' experiments. Marconi made equipment using directions in science magazines.

Those Handy Wright Brothers

To build their airplane, the Wright brothers used the following skills:

- carpentry (sawing, bending wood, hammering, etc.): to make the frame for their plane

- whittling: to shape the blades of the propellers

- tailoring (cutting, sewing): to make the cloth covering for the wings

- metal working: to build the engine

- photography: to record their experiments

Bonus: *Develop your handiness by studying books or TV programs about carpentry, sculpting, drawing, sewing, and model-making.*

PART 3

GET IDEAS

There is one thing stronger than all the armies in the world, and that is an idea whose time has come.
Victor Hugo

LEARN FROM ANIMALS

No animal ever got a patent. Still, animals "invented" all sorts of things before humans came up with the same ideas. Examples include jet propulsion (squid) and dam building (beavers).

Try this: *Write a report that compares an animal "invention" with its human counterpart. You might cover the following points:*

- *How the animal invention is like the human invention*
- *How the animal invention is different from the human invention*
- *The advantages of the animal invention*
- *The advantages of the human invention*

Bonus: *Choose an animal. Carefully study its behavior either by observing it first-hand or by reading about it or watching videos. See if the animal gives you an idea for an invention.*

Animal "Inventions"

air conditioning:	bee
basket weaving:	bird
body language:	bee
bridge building:	spider
camouflage:	moth
chemical warfare:	skunk
division of labor:	ant, bee
drinking straw:	mosquito
electric light:	lightning bug
fancy outfit:	peacock
farming:	ant
flight:	bat, bird
flipper:	frog
float:	jellyfish
glue:	spider
grooming:	chimpanzee
mobile home:	snail, crab
paper making:	wasp
porcupine:	pins
poison:	snake
rafting:	leaf-cutter ant
shower:	elephant
slavery:	ant
sonar:	bat
suction cup:	fly, octopus
teamwork:	lion, wolf
trapping:	spider
tunneling:	gopher
v-formation:	geese
war:	ant

★BIRDS AND THE AIRPLANE★

Probably the first person who saw a bird in flight thought, "I'd like to do that!" The dream appears in the ancient Greek myth "Daedelus and Icarus." A father and son make wings from bird feathers to escape a monster. Unhappily, Icarus flies too high. The sun melts the wax binding his wings, and the boy falls to his death.

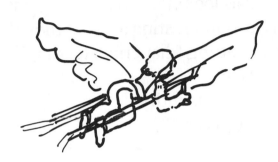

Birds did more than inspire stories. They served as models for inventors and scientists. In the 1500s, Leonardo da Vinci studied birds and used what he learned to sketch ideas for flying machines, but he never built one.

In 1894, *McClure's Magazine* published "The Flying Man," an article about Otto Lilienthal. Photos showed this daring German inventor soaring thirty feet high, hanging from a glider with bat-like wings. In Dayton, Ohio, Wilbur Wright read the article and began to think about making his own flying machine.

Wilbur spent many hours on his back, studying birds through binoculars. He noticed that they raised and lowered their wings when turning. This discovery led to the invention of an airplane wing whose shape could be changed in midair. The wing, patented in 1906, made human flight practical. Of course birds had been using the same idea for millions of years.

BE A PEOPLE WATCHER

If our lives always went along smoothly, there would be no need for inventions. But each day, big and little things go wrong. By noticing people in action, you can get ideas for all sorts of inventions.

Try this: *Pay attention to family members, friends, and neighbors. In your inventor's journal, list problems that they have and your ideas for solving them. For example, say that you're in a car. The driver wants to write down a phone number heard in a radio ad, but can't find paper or pencil. This may give you the idea for a note pad that sticks to the car's dash. Or how about a built-in tape recorder?*

What to Watch

Bird watchers like to watch birds build nests, hunt, soar, and feed their chicks. The list below may give you ideas for watching people. Hint: "People watching" includes listening as well as looking. What people say can be as interesting as what they do.

- baby-sitting (diapering, feeding)
- cooking
- doing the laundry
- driving a car
- gardening
- getting dressed
- house cleaning
- packing a suitcase
- playing games and sports
- reading a book or newspaper
- riding a bicycle
- talking on the phone
- watching TV

Bonus: *Watch yourself for a day or longer. List each action you do, such as: get up, brush teeth, put on socks, prepare a speech, practice a musical instrument, and so on. For each item, note any problems you have. Try to think of some way to make the task go easier, quicker, or better.*

★PROBLEM SOLVERS★

A Mom Who Made Millions

Ruth Handler noticed that her young daughter wanted to play with grown-up looking cutout dolls rather than with child-like dolls. Probably many parents saw the same thing. But Handler did something about it. Working with designers, she created a three-dimensional doll that could be dressed in stylish outfits. Experts at the 1959 New York Toy Show didn't think much of the idea. But within a decade "Barbie," named for the child who inspired it, earned half a billion dollars.

A Girl Who Saw Trouble and Did Something About It

In 1850, 12-year-old Margaret Knight visited the textile mill where her brother was working. She watched the shuttle zoom back and forth as it spooled out thread in a weaving machine. Then without warning, the shuttle flew out of the loom and injured a worker. Immediately, Margaret thought up a safety device that would keep the shuttle in its place and head off such accidents in the future. The idea worked, and was used in many mills.

A Boy Who Knew His Own Ears

Chester Greenwood lived in Farmington, Maine, where winter temperatures often dropped below freezing. When they did, Chester's ears turned blue and ached.

One day in 1873, 15-year-old Chester went ice skating. As usual, his ears hurt. Instead of ignoring them, he went home, twisted two pieces of wire into ear-size loops, and asked his grandmother to sew cloth onto them. When she was done, he snapped the loops over his ears and went outside.

Later, the young inventor added a spring-like strip of metal to hold the gadget onto his head. Many people in town wanted one, and soon Chester began selling his "Champion Ear Protectors."

Chester applied for a patent, which he received in 1877. When orders poured in, he opened a factory to manufacture what customers called "earmuffs."

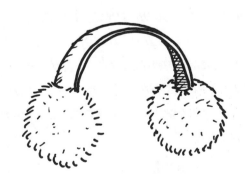

ENptJOY SURPRISES

When things don't work the way they're supposed to, some people get upset. But smart inventors take a second look. Curiosity can turn a mistake or unexpected result into a valuable product.

Try this: *Make a collection of "lucky" accident stories told by friends, family members, and neighbors. Ask them to describe how they turned something unexpected into something valuable.*

TWO "LUCKY" ACCIDENTS

Really Fast Food

In 1945, while experimenting with a high-energy radio tube, Percy Spencer found a melted candy bar in his pocket. He guessed that the magnetron tube had heated the candy. Spencer began a series of tests using electronic waves to quickly pop corn, cook eggs, and prepare other foods. The microwave oven had been born.

Moldy Wonder

In 1928, scientist Alexander Fleming was growing disease-causing bacteria. One day the bacteria unexpectedly began to die. Fleming soon found the cause, a mold that turned out to be a powerful bacteria fighter. The mold became the source of the world's first wonder drug, penicillin.

Bonus: *On the freeway, when cars smash together, it's a big mess. But some inventive person took that problem and created the "bumper car" ride that's so popular at amusement parks. Make a list of other kinds of accidents and disasters (floods, avalanches, etc.) and design a new amusement park ride. Describe your ride in pictures and words.*

★THE SLINKY STORY★

Wind and waves can toss ships around. The up-and-down and side-to-side motions cause seasickness. This rocking can also damage compasses and other important instruments.

During the 1940s, Richard James hoped to solve the problem. He knew that springs had long been used to smooth the ride of cars. Maybe metal coils could protect navigational devices.

One morning, while experimenting in his lab, James accidentally knocked a spring off a shelf. If it had fallen directly to the floor in a single leap, that might have been the end of the story. But this minor mishap turned out to be a fortunate fall.

The spring "sprang" from its starting place to a lower shelf. Instead of coming to a stop, it flipped forward and dropped toward a pile of books on a table. But it didn't rest there, either. The contraption somersaulted to the floor.

A less curious person might have picked up the spring and put it back on the shelf. But inventors are drawn to odd happenings. James began to conduct experiments, and found that the spring's amazing tumbling act wasn't a one-time thing. The snake-like device was good at all sorts of tricks, especially climbing down stairs.

Still, James wasn't sure that his invention had any value. Luckily, his wife Betty figured out that the spring was a new toy. She spent two days studying words in a dictionary until she found the right name for it: "Slinky." In 1946, the couple started a company, which now sells a million Slinkies a year.

Oddly, the toy that grew from serious research got back into the lab, this time in outer space. Astronauts aboard the space shuttle have used it to study gravity and wave motion.

THINK UP WILD IDEAS

Necessity is not the only mother of invention. Some inventors try to think up strange things just for the fun of it. For example, "What if a baseball had a light in it or made noise?"

Most "what if" ideas are silly and useless. But once in a while, what seems crazy at first turns out to be a valuable invention. (Sound-making baseballs now enable blind people to play the game.) That's why it makes sense to practice thinking the unthinkable.

Try this: *Pick a familiar object: book, TV, shoe, clock, banana, game board, etc. Brainstorm as many ways as possible for changing the thing. Think about:*

- *size*
- *color*
- *shape*
- *temperature*
- *number*
- *sound*
- *hardness*
- *action*

Don't worry about how the changes could actually be made. Simply let your mind work freely. Then pick the idea you like best. Name the new invention, draw it, and tell how it might be used.

What if . . .

- a week had nine days
- school lasted all year
- bicycles had five wheels
- TV was on just an hour a day
- kids ran the country
- you had one teacher for all the years you went to school
- you could order different colors of water from the water company

Bonus: *Describe a way to change the human body, for example, by adding a third eye. Explain the advantages and disadvantages of the change.*

★WILD INVENTIONS★

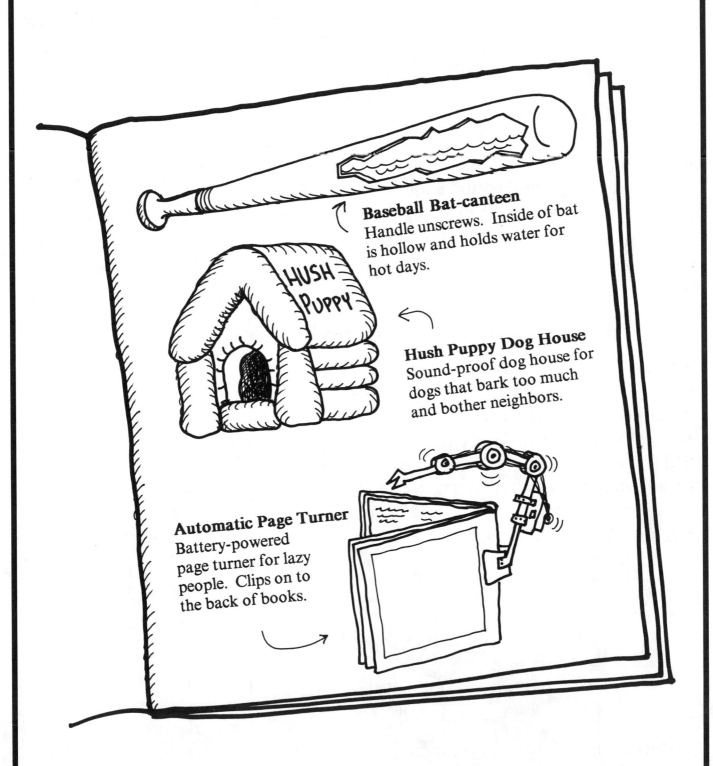

Baseball Bat-canteen
Handle unscrews. Inside of bat is hollow and holds water for hot days.

Hush Puppy Dog House
Sound-proof dog house for dogs that bark too much and bother neighbors.

Automatic Page Turner
Battery-powered page turner for lazy people. Clips on to the back of books.

RECYCLE THINGS

An invention can be something old used in a new way. For example, two buttons sewed onto a doll's head become eyes. The first person to do that was a real inventor.

So was George Washington Carver, the brilliant chemist who discovered hundreds of uses for peanuts, sweet potatoes, soybeans, and cotton waste. The demand for his new products created jobs for thousands of workers on farms and in factories while bettering people's lives around the world.

Try this: *Dream up new uses for each thing listed below. Hint: Think about using the things in games, to do chores, to make music, as hiding places, as toys, as costumes, and so on.*

- *book*
- *chewing gum*
- *strainer*
- *magnet*
- *milk carton*
- *rubber band*
- *paper clip*
- *pencil*
- *penny*
- *sock*

Drinking Glass Music Machine

Have you ever made music by running a wet finger around the edge of a drinking glass? Ben Franklin used that idea to invent the armonica. A foot pedal operated a device that turned the glasses. Two famous composers, Mozart and Beethoven, wrote music for it.

Bonus: *Brainstorm many different uses for an everyday object. Make a book that shows these inventions. Think up a catchy title like "Fifty Things To Do With a Cereal Box."*

★ WHAT CAN YOU DO WITH AN EGG? ★

SEED PLANTER

BIRD FEEDER

CHRISTMAS TREE ORNAMENTS

FUNNY MASK

HOUSE FOR BUGS

BATH TUB BOAT

S.S. EGG

IMITATE NATURE

Inventors have borrowed many ideas from nature. Sometimes the goal is to make a realistic copy, for example, artificial flowers. Other times, the aim is to imitate the way nature works, for example, to make a rainbow by making a glass prism. Copying nature may take years of observation and work. Examples include inventing the artificial heart, and developing the chess playing computer program.

Try this: *Study an invention based on nature. Examples are: fake gems, imitation wood, machine-made ice and snow, the robot arm, the roller coaster, and movie special effects (quicksand, volcanoes).*

Follow the steps that went into making the invention. Then compare the natural and the invented things. For example, artificial roses don't wilt.

Burrs and Velcro

In 1948, George de Mestral, a Swiss engineer, was hiking in the Alps. Along the way, burrs stuck to his pants. The problem wasn't new. But de Mestral suddenly wondered why the burrs stuck so well to fabric. Looking through a magnifying glass, he saw that tiny hooks on each burr clung to thread loops in the cloth.

The inventor thought that a burr-like fastener would be better than a button or zipper because it could be used with one hand. Years of research went into reaching that goal. The final product was made of tiny nylon hooks and loops.

Today, Velcro is found in jackets, shoes, luggage, space suits, and even artificial hearts.

Bonus: *Create an invention based on banana peels, eggshells, flowers, twigs, or other natural things. You might create something that looks like the original or that works like it.*

KNOW THE NEWS

The day's news is filled with stories about storms, accidents, and other disasters. No one likes bad news, but it can give inventors ideas for making the world a better place.

Try this: *Read a daily newspaper and watch TV news programs. In your inventor's diary, list problems that you learn about, and add your ideas for solving them.*

Christmas Tree Lights

During the early years of the twentieth century, many people used candles to decorate their Christmas trees. This was dangerous because the needles of a dry tree can quickly catch fire. In December, 1917, New York City newspapers reported that such a fire had killed four members of a family.

When 15-year-old Albert Sadacca learned about the tragedy, he had an idea. His parents had a business selling imitation birds in cages. In each bird was an electric light that made the bird glow. Albert's plan was to string similar bulbs together to replace candles on the trees. Electric lights would be easier to use, and safer.

Albert's parents liked the idea and began making the lights. The first year, they sold just one hundred strings, far fewer than they expected. But instead of quitting, Albert got an idea to improve the product. Instead of using plain glass, they'd paint the bulbs in bright colors. This did the trick. Albert eventually made a fortune while saving countless lives.

Bonus: *Explore your house, school, and town. Look for inventions that are meant to solve the kinds of problems you might see in the news, for example, smoke alarms. Choose one invention and research its history.*

COLLECT COMPLAINTS

Most people don't like listening to complaints. But complaints can inspire successful inventions. That's why you should pay attention when you hear others or yourself complaining.

THE FRIES ARE SOGGY!

In 1853, George Crum was a chef at the Moon Lake Lodge in Saratoga Springs, N.Y. A guest complained that the french fries were too thick and limp. To make fun of the guest, the chef sliced the next batch of potatoes as thin as he could and fried them so crisp, they snapped. Instead of being upset, the guest loved them. When others asked for the new treat, Crum started his own restaurant, which featured his invention: potato chips.

THE PANTS WEAR OUT TOO FAST!

In 1848, gold was discovered in California. Among the crowds coming west to seek riches was a cloth seller named Levi Strauss. In California he heard miners complaining that rocks in the gold fields tore their clothes. So Levi turned heavy canvas into extra-tough pants. Soon everyone wanted the pants, which came to be known as "Levi's."

Try this: *List your complaints about everyday objects. For example, maybe you dislike those little bits of rubber left after erasing. For each complaint, see if you can dream up an invention to solve the problem.*

Bonus: *Ask people you know—relatives, friends, and neighbors—to share their complaints with you. You might even set up a complaint box at school. Write the complaints in your inventor's notebook along with ideas for solving them.*

PART 4

INVENT FOR REAL

Everyone who's ever taken a shower has an idea. It's the person who does something about it who makes a difference.

Nolan Bushnell, inventor of Pong, the first popular video game

INVENT ADD-ON GADGETS

Many successful inventions are created by putting together two or more separate things. A few examples are: the lighted miner's hat, the alarm clock, talking movies (one company called them "radio pictures"), and peanut butter and jelly sandwiches.

Try this: *Dream up an add-on gadget by matching one thing in the first column with something else in the second. For example, a book with a heater built in might be perfect for reading outside on a cool evening. It's OK to use a thing more than once or to add items.*

Mix and Match

clock	bar of soap
fan	baseball
handle	book
heater	chair
light	doorknob
magnet	eyeglasses
magnifier	fork
name tag	leash
radio	pencil
recorder	postage stamp
smell	shoe
sound	umbrella
taste	wallpaper

WRITE IT RIGHT

Writing is one of the oldest and most valuable inventions. Throughout history, people have used all sorts of tools to write words: sticks, feathers and ink, even piles of stones. But no matter what they use, writers sometimes make mistooks.

In the 1800s, the lead pencil was becoming popular. The good news was that when people made mistakes, they could use pieces of latex (called "India rubber") to rub away their errors. The bad news was that erasers were easy to lose.

In 1858, H. L. Lipman of Philadelphia, Pennsylvania, solved the problem. Lipman attached a small holder at one end of a pencil. He then cemented a chunk of India rubber into the holder. By combining two old inventions, Lipman created the modern writing tool we all know and use. He also earned a fortune.

Today, Lipman's invention might seem like a simple idea. But that's true of many inventions . . . after they're invented.

Bonus: *Diagram one of your add-on inventions, and explain why it's a good idea.*

"TOOTHBRUSH TIMER" DINGS WHEN YOU HAVE BRUSHED LONG ENOUGH.

DING!

★BELLS AND WHISTLES★

Sometimes inventors will start with a simple product and add all sorts of extra features. For example, they might create a jump rope that glows in the dark and that makes a sound when its twirled. These kinds of extras are known as "bells and whistles" even when they don't make any noise. See how many bells and whistles you can count on the hat shown below.

DESIGN SOMETHING

Most inventions are meant to *do* something: an airplane flies, a refrigerator cools, an elevator lifts, a compass points, a mirror reflects, a scale weighs, a microscope magnifies. These are called utility inventions. "Utility" means "useful."

Another kind of invention focuses on how something *looks*. Imagine a toaster with one side made of clear plastic. The toaster works like a regular toaster. It just allows the owner to watch the bread darken. This kind of thing is called a design invention. It's meant to add beauty, fun, or interest to our world.

THE "HANDY" MUG

Try this: *Choose an everyday object such as a piece of clothing, a household product, a piece of jewelry, a sticker, something found at school, or a hobby-related item. Brainstorm several new designs for the thing. Think about:*
- *shape*
- *color*
- *size*
- *material or texture*
- *pattern*
- *add-on decorations*

Sketch each design. Then pick the one you like best.

Bonus: *Turn one of your designs into a working model. For example, design stationery for your family, an invitation for a party, a pin, or a T-shirt. Remember that the goal is not to change how the thing works, but only how it looks.*

DRINKING STRAWS IN THE SHAPE OF NAMES

★SAMPLE DESIGNS★

INVENT A GAME

Most games are like folk tales. Instead of having one inventor, they are created by many people over many years. For example, in the nineteenth century, football players played with a ball that was long and slender. Because it was hard to throw, most of the action involved running with the ball. In the 1930s, the shape was changed to make passing easier and more important.

Try this: *Choose a sport, a board game, or any other kind of game that you know a lot about. Experiment by changing one or more parts of the game. For example, what would happen in basketball if the net were twice as high? What if each team were allowed to put 10 players on the court? Or if players had to hop instead of run? Use the Game Planner to get more ideas. Write the rules and give the game a new name. Include a description of what it's like to play the new version of the game.*

Miniature Golf

No one is sure who invented golf, but we know the game was played in Scotland over 500 years ago. Because golf courses are big and require expensive care, the game was beyond the budget of many people.

In the 1920s, John Carter of Chattanooga, Tennessee, figured out how to solve that problem. To cut costs, he shrank the size of the playing area. This put the focus on putting, but lots of folks liked that part of the game best anyway.

Carter named his invention "Tom Thumb" golf, for a famous midget in P. T. Barnum's circus. The name didn't stick, but the game is more popular than ever.

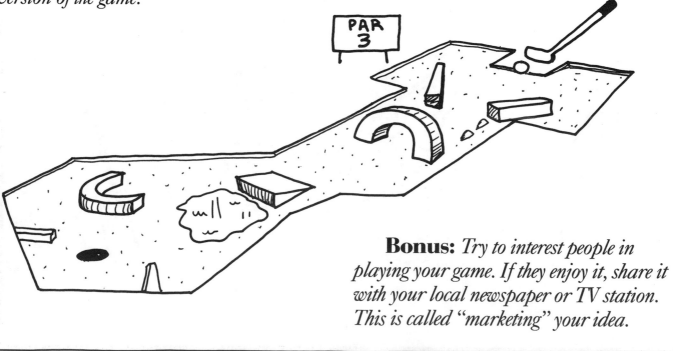

Bonus: *Try to interest people in playing your game. If they enjoy it, share it with your local newspaper or TV station. This is called "marketing" your idea.*

★GAME PLANNER★

The following suggestions won't work with every game.
Choose those that make sense for the game you're changing.
Add ideas of your own.

1. Change the number of players, for example, three-way checkers, or football with 20 players on a side.

2. Change the shape of the playing area, for cxample, five-base baseball or basketball played on a triangular court.

3. Change the size of the playing area, for example, human-sized chess.

4. Change the position of one or more players, for example, the pitcher in baseball pitches from the outfield.

5. Change the goal of the game, for example, in tennis the players see how long they can keep the ball in play.

6. Change the size of equipment, for example, playing Ping-Pong with grapefruit-sized Ping-Pong balls.

7. Change the time of play, for example, a basketball team has 10 seconds to shoot.

8. Limit the players in some way, for example, try "blindfold hopscotch."

INVENT A METHOD

People usually think of an invention as a gadget, like the can opener. But many inventions are methods, not objects.

A method is a way of doing a task. How you make a peanut butter sandwich is your method. Someone else might do it differently. Actors, artists, athletes, electricians, teachers, and other workers have methods for doing their jobs. Sometimes a person invents a method that is so much better than the old way, others in the field use it, too.

Try this: *Write a step-by-step description of a method that you use to do an everyday activity, such as:*
- *washing the dishes*
- *practicing a musical instrument*
- *memorizing spelling words*
- *studying a lesson at school*
- *shooting a free throw*

Examine each step and see if you can figure out a better way to do the job. Write the steps of the new method and test it out. If the method works, share it with others.

Famous Methods

- antiseptic surgery: Joseph Lister
- cooking scientifically: Fannie Farmer
- elementary education: Maria Montessori
- hydroponics (growing plants in water): William Gericke
- invention by teams: Thomas Edison
- making oxygen: Antoine Lavoisier
- mass production: Eli Whitney
- organizing library books: Melville Dewey
- piloting an airplane: Wright brothers
- realistic acting: Constantin Stanislavsky
- speed reading: Evelyn Woods
- vulcanizing rubber: Charles Goodyear

Bonus: *Read about the discovery of a famous method, for example, the invention of the curve ball in baseball. Or interview an expert about that person's method for doing something. It could be landing an airplane, painting a picture, or inventing a product.*

★TWO AMAZING METHODS★

The Apgar Score

"Birth," wrote Dr. Virginia Apgar, "is the most hazardous time of life." During the 1950s, Dr. Apgar began looking for a way to keep newborns from getting sick or dying. At that time, newborns were put in a blanket and taken to the nursery for later examination.

Dr. Apgar realized that if certain problems were detected and treated immediately after birth, many more infants would survive. She then developed a simple method for checking out babies on five points:

- pulse
- respiration
- muscle tone
- color
- reflexes

Her checklist, sometimes called "The Newborn Scoring System," has saved countless lives around the world.

The Fosbury Flop

Until the 1960s, high jumpers used the scissors method. They'd run at the bar, push off, and roll over face down. This seemed to be the natural way to jump. Most coaches taught it.

A high school athlete named Dick Fosbury tried jumping this way. But no matter how hard he practiced, he never won a prize.

Fosbury began to experiment. Instead of running straight to the bar, he followed a curved line, turned, and flipped backwards over the bar, with his face up.

Fans laughed because the "Fosbury Flop" looked odd. But at the 1968 Olympics, Fosbury won a gold medal with a record leap of seven feet four and a half inches. Soon jumpers everywhere studied his method. Eleven years later, Javier Sotomayor used it to break the "impossible" eight foot barrier.

INVENT A BUSINESS

A businessperson sells goods or services. The word "goods" means products like food, cars, clothing, and toys. The word "services" includes activities such as plumbing, cutting hair, and fixing cars.

There are two ways to invent a business. One is to think up a new method for selling a familiar product or service. For example, in 1933 Richard Hollingshead opened the first drive-in movie theater. Before then, people had to go inside to see a film. Now they could stay in their cars.

The other way to invent a business is to sell a new product or service. For example, in the 1980s, someone thought up the idea of the telephone wake-up call. For a small fee, customers would be awakened by a friendly voice rather than an alarm clock.

Try this: *Use the Business Planner to dream up a new kind of business. Share your plan with friends and with potential customers. See if people think you have a good idea.*

Selling "Parties"

In the 1930s, Earl Tupper invented machines to mold a new type of unbreakable plastic into bowls, cups, and other items. All had snap-on airtight lids. The product was a big hit.

But Tupper's most popular idea was yet to come. In 1951, he invented a new way to sell. He taught housewives how to throw selling parties at home. The plan worked so well, Tupper took his products out of regular stores. Soon others copied the idea of Tupperware Parties.

Bonus: *Most new businesses fail within the first year. To get tips for starting a successful business, interview someone who has kept a business going for several years. Also, read articles about new businesses. See if you can figure out why some succeed while others fail.*

★BUSINESS PLANNER★

Step 1. List your skills. Think about the skills you use in school, in hobbies, and around your home:

( ) acting
( ) baking, cooking
( ) computing
( ) drawing
( ) foreign language
( ) gardening

( ) musical
( ) photography
( ) sewing
( ) sports
( ) studying
( ) other

Step 2. Invent a way to use your skills to meet the needs of others. For example, if you know how to grow plants, you might create vegetable or flower gardens for other people. If you're good with a camcorder, you might make video diaries of babies.

Step 3. Decide how much to charge customers for your goods or services. Think about the materials you'll need. Will you need others to help you get the work done? You might talk to people who run similar businesses.

Step 4. Give your business a name that's easy to remember.

Step 5. Go over your business plan with an adult to see if it makes sense and is safe. Check with city hall to find out if you need to get a permit.

Step 6. Advertise by posting flyers. You might also write or phone the local newspaper and TV station to suggest that a reporter do a story about your business.

INVENT A CHARACTER

Telling stories is one of the most important human activities. The first step in creating a good story is inventing an interesting character: either a person or a thing that acts like a person, for example, a talking animal.

Try this: *Invent a character for a story or to stand for something you believe in. For example, Smokey Bear stands for taking care of our forests. The questions below can help you create your character.*

Questions For Creating a Character

- If you had to describe the character in one word, what would it be?
- What is the character's most important skill?
- What is the character's main goal or interest?
- If the character were allowed to say one sentence, what would it be?
- What kind of friends does the character have?
- What is the character's most important possession?
- What is the character's most noticeable physical quality?
- What is special about the character's clothing?

I NEED YOU!

Bonus: *List five or ten characters that interest you. They might come from stories, for example, King Kong, Snoopy, Frankenstein, Mickey Mouse, or E.T. Or they might be symbols, for example, Uncle Sam or a character from a commercial. Pick one and use the character questions (above) to see what makes him or her interesting. Or do library research to discover how the character came to be.*

★THE INVENTION OF SANTA CLAUS★

Once upon a time, Santa Claus was a real person. His name was Nicholas, a bishop who lived in Asia Minor (now Turkey). Nicholas devoted his life to helping others. The name "Saint Nicholas" became "Sint Nocoles" in Germany and "Sinterklass" in Holland. It ended up "Santa Claus" in English-speaking places.

In 1823, a biblical scholar and poet named Clement Moore wrote the now-famous Christmas poem "A Visit from St. Nicholas." In that poem, Moore described Santa Claus as a "jolly old elf." The poem was so widely loved that most artists who drew or painted Santa after that time pictured him as elfish.

In 1930, the Coca-Cola Company's advertising manager, Archie Lee, decided to use Santa Claus in holiday advertising. He hired Haddon Sundblom, a Chicago artist, to paint a Santa. Sundblom's Santa was a big, warm, friendly character.

As a model, the painter used a retired salesman named Lou Prentice, a man whose face was lined with happy wrinkles. Many years later, when Sundblom had aged enough, he used his own face for a model.

The Santa that appeared in the Coca-Cola advertisements became well-known over the years. Now almost everybody's idea of Old Saint Nick looks like Sundblom's pictures.

BORROW AN INVENTION

Many inventions are based on old ideas. For example, in 1859, the idea of the ship's propeller was used to make a propeller for an airship. In 1882, the propeller was used to make the electric fan. And then, in 1903, the Wright brothers used propellers on their airplane. Each time propellers did the same kind of work: pushing something, either water or air. This kind of inventing is called "adapting."

Try this: *Make a list of ordinary things around your house, for example, broom, tea bag, toothbrush, window shade, soap dish, toothpaste tube, vacuum cleaner. For each item, think up a place where that thing could do its job in a new way.*

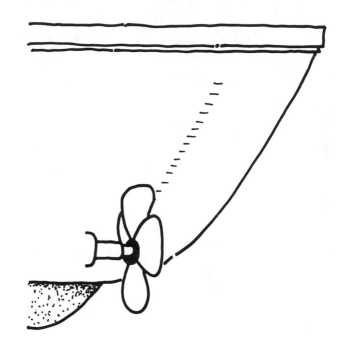

Bonus: *Read about an invention that was created from an earlier product. Examples include:*
* *sewing → surgical stitches*
* *flip books → motion pictures*
* *drive-through bank → drive-through fast-food restaurant*
* *snow skis → water skis*
* *hand mirror → car rearview mirror*

★FROM HORSEBACK TO THE MOON★

A thousand years ago, Arab riders played a game called "Little War." They chased each other in a circle, while playing catch with perfume-filled clay balls. A rider would lose if a ball hit and doused him with perfume. Around the year 1100, European Crusaders (religious soldiers) invaded Arab lands. When they returned home, they took the idea of "Little War" home with them.

By 1500, the game was played in France, Italy, and Spain, where it was called carosella, Spanish for "Little War." Riders decorated their horses and wore fancy costumes. But instead of catching balls, they tried to spear rings hung from poles while musicians made music. In 1680, a teacher in France invented a machine to train riders. He hung wooden horses from a long bar attached to a pole. Helpers pushed the bar to make the horses go around in a circle as riders tried to catch the rings. In 1729, George Stevens wrote a poem about these "merry-go-rounds."

Another Frenchman added pedals to the horses. The harder that riders pedaled, the faster the merry-go-round moved. The pedal carousel was a hit at fairs. Then an Englishman created a steam-driven carousel that also had a pipe organ. Roofs were added. In 1915, electricity was used to drive the machines.

Later, the merry-go-round idea was adapted as a rotating food-serving invention called a "lazy susan." Then it inspired the "baggage carousel" found at airports on earth and, in a silly TV commercial, at a rocketport on the moon.

IMPROVE AN INVENTION

In 1876, Alexander Graham Bell invented the telephone. At first it had no dial. To make a call, customers turned a crank to ring up an operator. The operator then made the connection. Many inventors helped change Bell's creation. First, the rotary dial was added so that calls could be made without an operator. Later, push buttons replaced the dial to make phoning quicker. In the 1960s came the videophone, and in the 1980s, the cellular phone, which lets people call from cars, boats, planes, and even bicycles.

Each of the changes in the telephone is called an "improvement." Making improvements is a common kind of inventing, and plays a major role in shaping the things in our lives, from food to clothes to computers.

Try this: *Choose an invention from around your house or school. It should be something that you often use, for example, a pencil sharpener, a vegetable peeler, or a toy. Look for ways that the thing could be made better. Think about changing the thing using one or more of the ideas listed in the box. Describe the changes in your notebook.*

Kinds of Improvements

- Safety: Can it be made less dangerous to use?
- Size: Would it be better if it were larger or smaller?
- Strength: Do parts often break?
- Noise: Is it too loud?
- Sound: Does it need a sound?
- Looks: Could it be prettier?
- Ease: Could it be easier to use?
- Cost: Could it be made cheaper?
- Speed: Could it work faster?
- Weight: Should it be lighter or heavier?

Bonus: *Interview an adult about how one thing has been improved during that person's life. Topics might be: airplanes, cars, TV, highways, refrigerators, movies, medicine, sports, or telephones.*

INVENT A GROUP

Groups or clubs devoted to things like scouting, photography, and ecology don't just happen. They're invented. One or a few people get the idea and then bring other interested people together. Clubs can be for fun or for dealing with emergencies and other serious matters.

Creating a Group

No two groups are exactly alike, but here are some points to think about when planning your group:
- Name of group
- Purpose
- Activities
- Who can join (age, skills, etc.)
- Uniform or costume
- Motto
- Pledge or oath
- Song or anthem
- Rules

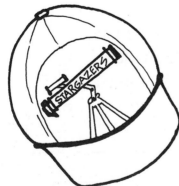

Bonus: *Use your imagination to invent a group that might exist in the future. It could be for robots, time travelers, people who vacation on distant planets, or any other group that doesn't exist yet.*

Try this: *Think up an idea for a club or group. It might relate to a hobby, a topic (flying saucers or dinosaurs), a skill (whistling), or community service (painting murals). Make a booklet that describes the group. If you like your plan, see if other people will help turn it into reality.*

The American Red Cross

After seeing the horrors of war in 1859, Henry Dunant, a Swiss citizen, got the idea for a group that would help those in need everywhere. In 1864, people from 16 countries met in Geneva, and chose the red cross as a symbol of neutral aid. (The red crescent became the symbol of aid in Muslim countries.)

During the American Civil War, a woman named Clara Barton served as a nurse. Known as the "Angel of the Battlefield," she later brought aid to people in the Franco-Prussian War.

In 1881, Barton organized the American Red Cross. During the next quarter of a century, she built this life-saving group into one of the most important charities in America.

INVENT A TOY

Toys aren't just for fun. They're also learning tools. For example, a toy gyroscope teaches about gravity, and a pogo stick offers practice in balance

Try this: *Invent a toy. To start your ideas flowing, take a walk through a toy store or read a few books about toys.*

TOY MAKING TIPS

• **Choose your audience.** Making a toy is like writing a story. You have to know who will use your invention. Just watching kids play can give you many ideas for toys. Hint: pay attention to what kids do: build, climb, pretend to be an astronaut, and so on.

• **Think about different kinds of toys.**
Models: dolls, tin soldiers, dinosaurs, cars
Tools: chemistry set, play stethoscope, telescope
Materials: clay, building blocks, paints, magnets
Equipment: things to throw, things to play with
Costumes: masks, hats, badges

• **Brainstorm real-world things that your toy can imitate.** For example, if you like water slides, you could make a water slide toy.

• **Sketch the toy.** Think about how it will be used, how big it should be, and what it might be made of.

• **Create a working model and test it.** Give extra attention to safety. For example, little kids often choke on parts of toys that come loose.

Bonus: *Research the history of a toy, such as Erector Set, Lego Blocks, Lincoln Logs, Tinker Toys, or the kaleidoscope. Besides reading books, you could send a research letter to a toy company. You can find addresses on toy boxes, or by asking someone at a toy store.*

PART 5

SHARE YOUR IDEAS

No one is useless in this world who
lightens the burdens of another.
Charles Dickens

"THE ROCKET"

1829
STEAM ENGINE

LEARN ABOUT PATENTS

A patent is a government report that uses words and pictures to describe an invention. The patent gives the inventor the right to make, use, or sell the invention for a set time, usually 17 years. During this period, no one else may use the idea unless the inventor agrees.

The word "patent" means open. A patent is open for anyone to read. While people can't use a patented idea without permission, reading about it may inspire other inventions. In fact, encouraging new ideas is a major reason for having a patent system.

Try this: *Study the page from the patent for the Slinky. See if you can find the following information:*
- *Date of the patent*
- *Patent number*
- *Official title of the patent*
- *Inventor's name*
- *Inventor's signature*

Bonus: *Order and study the patent of an invention that interests you. Send three dollars to the Commissioner of Patents & Trademarks, Box 9, Washington, D.C. 20231. You'll need the patent number. Sometimes it's printed on the invention. If not, you may get it by writing the company that makes the thing. Five famous patent numbers are: 1647 (telegraph), 6281 (safety pin), 174,465 (telephone), 821,393 (the airplane), and 2,524,035 (transistor).*

The Inventor President

In 1790, Thomas Jefferson created the U.S. patent system. He was the country's first patent examiner. In that job he decided whether or not an invention was new enough to be protected by a patent. Jefferson himself had invented a swivel chair, a pedometer, a camp stool, and a copying device, the "polygraph."

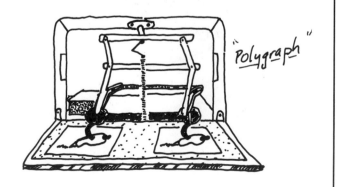

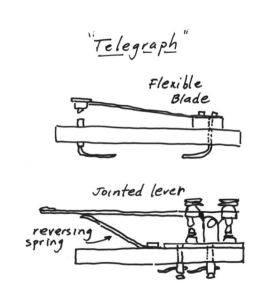

★PAGE FROM THE SLINKY PATENT★

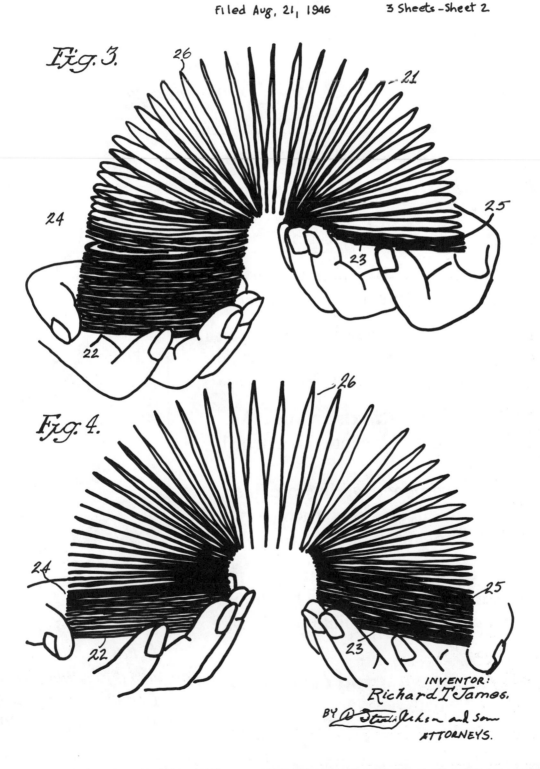

Jan. 28, 1947.

R. T. JAMES
TOY AND PROCESS OF USE
Filed Aug. 21, 1946

2,415,012

3 Sheets—Sheet 2

Fig. 3.

Fig. 4.

INVENTOR:
Richard T James.
BY .... and Son
ATTORNEYS.

APPLY FOR A PATENT

To get a patent, you must describe your invention in an application sent to the Patent and Trademark Office. If the patent officials think your idea is new, they will issue a patent. Otherwise, they will reject the idea or ask for more information. Even a good idea might be turned down at first. This happened to the Wright brothers!

Try this: *Pretend you invented a familiar thing, such as the safety pin or the wrist watch. Draw several pictures of the thing showing what it is and how it works. Label each drawing in order using the words "Figure 1," "Figure 2," etc. Then follow the steps in the box to describe the thing as if you were applying for a patent.*

Describing an Invention

1. Name the invention. The title should be clear and short. For this practice, give the old thing you're working with a new name.

2. Give background information. Tell what type of invention you have (toy, tool, etc.).

3. Briefly describe the invention. In a few sentences, tell what it is and how it solves problems that earlier inventions didn't solve.

4. List and name the drawings. For example, if your pretend invention is a pencil, your list might be:
Figure 1: Unsharpened writing machine
Figure 2: Sharpened writing machine
Figure 3: Writing machine held in hand

5. Give a detailed description of the invention and how it works. This should be so clear that any expert in the field could make and use it.

6. List exactly what you claim as your discovery. Tell what's new.

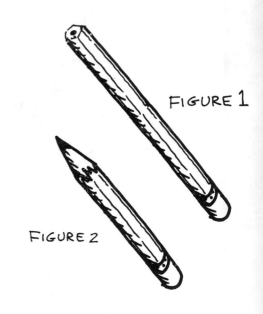

FIGURE 1

FIGURE 2

Bonus: *Write a patent for one of your own ideas. It could be for something real or fantastic. For information about fees, and forms, write to: Commissioner of Patents, Washington, D.C. 20231.*

★A STIRRING AND EATING TOOL★

BACKGROUND

This invention is a cooking and eating device. Its main use relates to liquid and soft foods. Stirring and eating with fingers can be messy and even painful if the food is hot. My invention solves these problems.

SUMMARY OF THE INVENTION

The stirring and eating tool does the same work that the hand does when it takes a cup-like shape. Unlike the hand, which is covered with delicate skin, the stirring and eating tool is made of materials not easily harmed by heat. It can also be made in many sizes.

BRIEF DESCRIPTION OF THE DRAWINGS

Figure 1 is a view from above.
Figure 2 is a view of the tool used for stirring.
Figure 3 is a view of the tool used for eating.

DETAILED DESCRIPTION

The spoon consists of a handle (Figure 1A) and a bowl (Figure 1B). It can be made of wood, metal, or plastic. The bowl can be shallow if the main purpose is stirring (Figure 2). Or it can be made deep for eating (Figure 3). The size of the handle and the bowl can vary. For example, a long handle might be best for stirring liquids in deep pots. A shorter handle would be easier to use for eating soups, cereals, and so on. A version of the device with holes or slots in the bowl could be used for separating objects (for example, meat balls) from liquids.

CLAIMS

I claim a stirring and eating tool which resembles the cupped hand but which is made from more durable materials.

I also claim a straining tool which resembles the cupped hand with fingers slightly separated.

★PATENT FACTS AND TIPS★

The world's first patent was issued in Venice in 1474. The first U.S. patent went to Sam Hopkins for a new way to make potash, used in soap and fertilizer.

In 1880 the Patent Office quit asking for working models. They no longer had room to store them!

Experts can usually tell if an invention will work by studying the inventor's words and drawings. The only type of patent application that must include a working model is a perpetual motion device, a machine that works without using fuel. Scientists don't think such a machine is possible, so they insist on seeing one work before they will read an application for such an invention.

In 1900 President McKinley said, "Everything that can possibly be invented has been invented." This was before the airplane, radio, TV, nuclear power, personal computer, space shuttle, laser, and millions of other inventions.

In 1980 Ananda Chakrabarty won the first patent on a living thing, a microbe that breaks down oil.

In the U.S., nearly 200,000 patent applications are filed yearly, and about 100,000 patents are granted. More than five million U.S. patents have been issued since 1790.

Thomas Edison holds the record for number of patents: 1093.

You can be an inventor without getting a patent. A famous example is Ben Franklin. Franklin believed that some inventions, such as his lightning rod, were too important for anyone to own, even the inventor.

If you get an idea for improving a company's product, instead of seeking a patent, you can write to the company and tell them you have an idea. Some companies will consider ideas from outsiders and will send you a special form to sign. This can protect you and the company.

INVENTOR'S ADDRESS BOOK

Writing letters can play a role in inventing. When Wilbur and Orville Wright were developing the airplane, they exchanged hundreds of letters with fellow inventors and with family members. They also wrote to businesses to get facts about parts and materials, for example, an engine to power their plane.

Sharing ideas and questions with people you trust can help you succeed as an inventor. Here are a few addresses you might use to start your inventor's address book. As you find people who are interested in your work, add their names.

Warning: You may read advertisements for companies that claim to help inventors sell their ideas. Many of these companies don't really help. They're just interested in taking money from inventors. Be careful!

Invention Contests

Invent America
510 King Street, Suite 420
Alexandria, VA 22314
Grades K-8, Deadline:
April 1

Weekly Reader
   National Inventive
   Thinking Contest
245 Long Hill Road
Middletown, CT 06457
Grades K-6, Deadline:
Early in March

American Inventor Network
6770 Depot Street
Sebastopol, CA 95472

American Society of Inventors
Box 58426
Philadelphia, PA 19102

Government Printing Office
710 N. Capitol Street
Washington, D.C. 20401

Inventors' Workshop International
3201 Corte Malpaso, Suite 304
Camarillo, CA 93010

Library of Congress
101 Independence Avenue SE
Washington, D.C. 20540

Minnesota Inventors' Congress
Box 71
Redwood Falls, MN 56283

National Air and Space Museum
Washington, D.C. 20560

National Assn. of Manufacturers
1331 Pennsylvania Avenue NW
Washington, DC 20504-1703

National Invention Center
80 West Bowery Suite 201
Akron, Ohio 44308

Patent and Trademark Office
Washington, D.C. 20231

Smithsonian Institution
Washington, D.C. 20560

READING LIST

Many inventors got their start by reading popular science magazines, and invention related books, such as those listed here.

INVENTORS AND INVENTIONS

The Inventive Yankee (Yankee Books, 1989). Origins of the submarine, roller skates, and other New England creations.

Outward Dreams: Black Inventors and Their Inventions by Jim Haskins (Walker, 1991). Lives of dozens of important but frequently forgotten innovators.

Small Inventions That Make a Big Difference (National Geographic, 1984). Stories behind the aqua-lung, barbed wire, cement, fireworks, and other important creations.

The Smithsonian Book of Invention (Norton, 1978). Everything from the first stone axe to the space shuttle.

Steven Caney's Invention Book (Workman, 1985). Presents projects, plus stories of 35 inventions.

Weird & Wacky Inventions by Jim Murphy (Crown, 1978). Visual puzzles feature odd-looking but actual inventions.

Why Didn't I Think of That? From Alarm Clocks to Zippers by Webb Garrison (Prentice-Hall, 1977). Often-surprising histories of everyday objects.

The Wright Brothers: How They Invented the Airplane by Russell Freedman (Holiday House, 1991). The story of the Wright brothers' triumph, featuring photos taken by the brothers.

SKILLS AND PROCESSES

Hammer & Saw: An Introduction to Woodworking by Harvey Weiss (Crowell, 1981). This practical little book covers many carpentry basics. The simple text and clear pictures encourage handiness.

How a House Happens by Jan Adkins (Walker, 1972). Shows a house taking shape from first rough drawings through the final painting. A useful resource for inventing houses of the future.

How Things Are Made (National Geographic, 1981). Clear text and large, colorful photographs show the steps in making familiar objects.

How Things Work (National Geographic Society, 1983). Uses photographs, drawings, and words to take readers inside many different inventions.

Louisville Slugger: The Making of a Baseball Bat by Jan Arnow (Pantheon, 1984). From tree to finished bat, the book illustrates what manufacturing is all about.

Metals by Robin Kerrod (Silver Burdett, 1981). Basic manufacturing processes including molding, rolling, forging, pressing, stamping, drawing, extruding, cutting, joining, and decorating.

Patent It Yourself by David Press (Nolo Press, 1991). Covers all steps for patenting, and includes all necessary forms.

TEACHER TIPS

Each self-contained activity in *How to Be an Inventor* offers step-by-step directions that guide students through a key activity and a bonus project. In most cases, a follow-on page provides a model or related resource. With young children, you can present the material orally. For able readers, photocopy the pages and have your young inventors work individually or in small groups.

The following activities are meant to create a climate that nurtures interest in invention and that reinforces the ideas found in the book.

Read aloud from books about inventors: Highlight specific qualities, such as persistence. Choosing passages from a book like Autumn Stanley's *Mothers and Daughters of Invention* (Scarecrow Press) will enable you to celebrate the contributions of often ignored inventors.

Make time lines: Possible themes:
- Inventions through history (agriculture, transportation, communications, etc.)
- Inventions of your state or province
- Inventions made during the students' lifetime (or parents' lifetime)

Map inventions: Have students find the origins of such inventions as instant coffee (Switzerland), the radio (Italy), pasta (China), alphabetic writing (Egypt), the railroad (England), TV (U.S.), neon light (France), democracy (Greece), and so on.

Take field trips: Visit places where all sorts of products are manufactured. Ask the experts to explain such basic processes as: molding, extruding, grinding (use of lathes), die-cutting, and stamping. Focus also on the nature of materials used: wood, plastic, glass, steel, and so on.

Enter contests: (See Inventor's Address Book, page 77.)

Invite guest speakers: Find local inventors by contacting inventor clubs or patent attorneys, or posting notices in the library. Ask the speaker to tell the story behind an invention and answer questions. Guests who repair products can share secrets of engines, airplanes, faucets, vacuum cleaners, copy machines, locks, and bicycles. Knowing how old inventions work can spark ideas for dreaming up new ones.

Make models: Teach handiness by having students create replicas of the frisbee, the Wrights' airplane, and other things. Use clay, balsa, and other inexpensive materials.

Assign reports: Have students report on school-related inventions: bells, chalk, chalkboard, computers, the Dewey Decimal system, flag, games, holidays (origin of Mother's Day), maps, and writing implements.

Study simple machines: Many inventions consist of one or more of five classic machines. Have kids experiment with the lever, pulley, inclined plane, screw, and wheel-and-axle.

Create a hall of fame: Have students make posters of their favorite inventions and inventors.

INDEX

Accidents, lucky, 44, 45
Adapting, 66, 67
Addresses, 77
Airplane, 9, 13, 26, 27, 31, 38, 41
Amusement park rides, 44
Analysis, 24, 25
Animals, 40, 41
Apgar, Virginia, 61
Barbie Doll, 43
Barton, Clara, 69
Baseball, 19
Bell, Alexander, 68
Bells and Whistles, 55
Bicycle, 17
Bird watching, 41
Black inventors, 48, 78
Braille, 33
Brainstorming, 48, 49
Bushnell, Nolan, 53
Business, invent a, 62, 63
Carousel, 67
Carver, George W., 48
Character, invent a, 64, 65
Christmas tree lights, 51
Club, invent a, 69
Collaboration, 30, 31
Combining things, 54, 55
Complaints, 52
Contests, 77
Creative thinking, 46-49
Critical thinking, 34, 35
Curie, Marie, 5, 28
Current events, 51
Da Vinci, Leonardo, 12, 41
Design inventions, 56, 57
Drawing, 22, 23
Earmuffs, 43
Edison, Thomas, 21, 76
Evaluate an invention, 35
Experimenting, 29, 38

Fact finding, 27
Failure, 36, 37
Farnsworth, Philo, 15
Fast-food restaurant, 37
Fleming, Alexander, 44
Fosbury Flop, 61
Franklin, Ben, 48, 76
Frisbee, 33
Gadgets, 54, 55
Games, 58, 59
Goddard, Robert, 10
Guillotine, 33
Handiness, 24, 25, 38
Handler, Ruth, 43
High jump, 61
Hugo, Victor, 39
Icarus and Daedelus, 41
Improve inventions, 16, 68
Interview an inventor, 20
Invention process, 9, 10
Invention safari, 18
Inventor qualities, 6
Inventor study chart, 14
Inventor's diary, 11-13
Inventors, list of, 15, 28
James, Richard/Betty, 45
Jefferson, Thomas, 72
Journal, 11
Letter writing, 26, 27
Levi's, 52
Lilienthal, Otto, 41
Lucky accidents, 44, 45
Manufacturing, 25
Marconi, Guglielmo, 9, 38
Marketing, 32, 33, 62, 63
McDonald's, 37
Merry-go-round, 67
Method, invent a, 60, 61
Microwave oven, 44
Miniature golf, 58
Models, 38

Motion Pictures, 9
Naming a product, 32, 33
NASA, 20, 37
Nature, imitate, 50
Necessity, 37, 52
Notebook, 11
Observation, 40-43
Organization, invent a, 69
Patents, 72-76
Pencil with eraser, 54
Penicillin, 44
People watching, 42, 43
Plastic, 33
Potato chips, 52
Quiz, 7, 8
Radio, 9, 38
Recycling things, 48, 49, 66, 67
Red Cross, 69
Research, 9, 26, 27, 40-43
Safety pin, 10
Santa Claus, 65
Scavenger hunt, 18
Science, 28, 29
Scientific method, 29
Slinky, 45, 73
Smithsonian Institution, 26
Steps of invention, 9, 10
Superman, 37
Teamwork, 30, 31
Telephone, 68
Toys, 70
Tupperware parties, 62
Utility vs. design, 56
Velcro, 50
Whitney, Eli, 60
Women inventors, 15, 20, 28, 37, 43, 45, 61, 69
Wright brothers, 9, 13, 26, 27, 28, 38, 41
Zipper, 32

HOW TO BE AN INVENTOR